ABC

Dessert Book

AO PRESS

Jessica Lee Anderson

Paperback ISBN: 978-1-964078-03-8

Photo credits—Front cover: A: Billion Photos (Strawberry Ice Cream), B: DAPA Images (Vanilla Ice Cream), C: ValentynVolvok (Blue Ice Cream), Ruth Black, GW from wonwage; Back Cover: Ruth Black; Cover Page: A: Flip Side (Strawberry Pie), B: Magone (Whipped Cream Dessert), C: Tatiana7744 (Chocolate Cake), DAPA Images (Berry on Layered Cake); Copyright Page: Ruth Black (Cake Pops); Dedication Page: Kzenon (Pastry Shop); p. 4: A: NNehring (Apple Crisp), Donyype, Joe Lena, bhofack2; p. 5: B: jirkaejc (Bundt Cake), pixelshot, Yana Tatevosian, TorriPhoto; p. 6: Billion Photos (Cupcake), Magone, Geo's Gallery, mvp64; p. 7: D: tirc83 (Dundee Cake), bonchan, bhofack2, Grace Studio; p. 8: E: Sandra Backwinkel (Eggnog Cake), ddukang, Alisa Farov, Yevhen Roshchyn; p. 9: F: kttpngart (Fruit Cake), welcomia, Miguel Soutull, jenifoto; p. 10: G: bhofack2 (Gooey Butter Cake), Windawake, Annapolis Studios, Angela Medler; p. 11: H: fasphotographic (Hot Cross Buns), Megan Betz, Brand X Pictures, lauraag; p. 12: I: tornado98 (Italian Cream Cake), gingagi, Meem Images, VeselovaElena; p. 13: J: Oleksandr Prokopenko (Jam Tart), eddtoro, seramo, Kate Smirnova; p. 14: K: ClarkandCompany (Kransekage), JMichl, keko64, Jenniveve84; p. 15: L: davidf (Lamingtons), voltan1, annie-claude, pixelshot; p. 16: M: Quiet Josephine (Mississippi Mud Pie), DAPA Images, Lauri Patterson, Kue Madeleine; p. 17: N: chas53 (Nutty Fudge Brownies), rolbos, rimmabondarenko, Ahanov Michael; p. 18: O: vikif (Orange Sherbet), boblin, Jordanlye, pitpilai; p. 19: P: gsagi (Pecan Pie), Brand X Pictures, MSPhotographic, Billion Photos; p. 20: Q: Eva-Katalin (Queen of Pudding), Artem Bolshakov, Nataliaspb, Janna Danilova; p. 21: R: Kristin Utzinger (Rainbow Sherbet); Estefania Vizcaino, Andrei Ureche; p. 22: S: NRedmond (Sweet Potato Pie), Olga Miltsova, Tatyana Consul, Debbi Smirnoff; p. 23: T: Monkey Business Images (Treacle Tart), jmsilva, letty17, bloodstone; p. 24: U: Candice Bell (Ube Cake Roll), bhofack2, Vania Ribejro, darkscott; p. 25: V: bhofack2 (Vanilla Custard), Ninikas, ac_bnphotos, Rocky89; p. 26: W: Margoe Edwards (White Chocolate Chip Cookie), bonchan, Nadezhda_Nesterova, DariolaVera; p. 27: X: daoloduc (Xoi La Cam), bernashafo, lermont51, ancoay; p. 28: Y: pixelshot (Yorkshire Pudding), Vsandandhakrishna, arinahabich, Griffin24; p: 29: Z: lesyy (Zabaglione), Debbi Smirnoff, enzodebernardo, A-Lein, p. 30: asofa, Elisabeth Coelfen, Denys Gromov, gmnicholas; p. 31: Michael Anderson

This Book Belongs to:

_____

A is for . . .

Apple Pie

Almond Cookies

Angel Food Cake

A a

 **is for . . .**

Brownies

Banana Cream Pie

Black Forest Cake

B b

5

C is for . . .

Cheesecake

Chocolate Chip Cookie

Carrot Cake

C c

 **is for . . .**

Dirt Pudding

Devil's Food Cake

Donuts

E is for . . .

Eclair

Egg Custard
Tarts

Elephant Ear Pastries

E e

8

F is for . . .

Fruit Tart

Flan

Funnel Cake

F f

9

G is for . . .

Gingerbread House

Grasshopper Pie

German Chocolate Cake

G g

 **is for . . .**

Hot Fudge Sundae

Huckleberry Pie

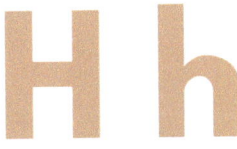

Hummingbird Cake

I is for . . .

Iced Lemon Pound Cake

Ice Cream Cone

Ice Cream Cake

Ii

 **is for . . .**

Jaffa Cakes

Jelly Roll

Jam Bars

J j

13

K is for . . .

Kiwifruit Tart

Key Lime Pie

King Cake

K k

14

 **is for . . .**

Lava Cake

Lemon Bars

Lemon Meringue Pie

L l

 **is for . . .**

Macarons

Macaroons

Madeleines

M m

16

 **is for . . .**

Nectarine Cobbler

Neapolitan Ice Cream

Napoleon Cake

N n

O is for . . .

Oatmeal Cookies

Opera Cake

Orange Cake

 **P** is for . . .

Peanut Butter Cookies

Peach Crisp

Pumpkin Pie

P p

Q is for . . .

Qurabiya

Queen Cake

Quince Tarte Tatin

Q q

 **R** is for . . .

Rice Pudding

Red Velvet Cake

Rhubarb Pie

 **R r**

21

S is for . . .

Sugar Cookies

S'mores

Strawberry Shortcake

S s

T is for . . .

Tiramisu

Tres Leches Cake

Trifle

T t

23

U is for . . .

Ube Ice Cream

Unicorn Cake

Upside Down Cake

U u

V is for . . .

Vanilla Ice Cream

Victoria Sponge Cake

Vegan Mousse

V v

W is for . . .

Whoopie Pie

Watermelon Sorbet

Wedding Cake

W w

 **X** is for . . .

Xocai Chocolate Mug Cake

Xylitol Pudding

Xuixo Pastry

 **X x**

 is for . . .

Yogurt Soft-Serve

Yellow Butter Cake

Yule Log

 **is for . . .**

Zeppola

Zucchini Chocolate Bundt Cake

Zebra Cake

Z z

5 Dessert Facts:

 Cake is one of the most popular desserts of all time, and it is usually topped with sweet icing.

 Cookies are usually flat and round, and some varieties can be cut into fancy shapes.

 Pastries such as pies and tarts have a flaky crust and are filled with things like cream, fruit, chocolate, or nuts.

Some desserts are deep-fried like donuts or frozen like ice cream or milkshakes.

 Desserts can be made with sugar substitutes like xylitol (which can be toxic to dogs).

Jessica Lee Anderson is an award-winning author of over 75 books for young readers. Jessica lives near Austin, Texas with her daughter, Ava, and husband, Michael. Gluten free cake is one of Jessica's favorite desserts. You can learn more about Jessica by visiting www.jessicaleeanderson.com.

Check out these other titles:

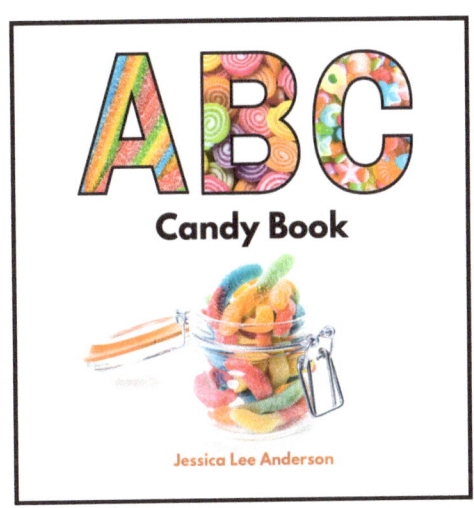

www.ingramcontent.com/pod-product-compliance
Lightning Source LLC
Chambersburg PA
CBHW041500120626
46547CB00003B/494